About the Author

Born in Newcastle upon Tyne, Garfield Taylor grew up in Corbridge, a village on the river Tyne in Northumberland. He attended Sedbergh School (now in Cumbria) and, following that, Rutherford College in Newcastle. He then joined Lloyds Bank, gaining his AIB (Associate of the Institute of Bankers) and worked in various branches in northeast England. He is now retired and lives in Scarborough, dedicating his time to seeing family members, reading, motoring and writing poetry.

WHITE HORSES
A Collection of Poems

GARFIELD TAYLOR

First published in Great Britain in 2016 by
The Book Guild Ltd
9 Priory Business Park
Wistow Road, Kibworth
Leicestershire, LE8 0RX
Freephone: 0800 999 2982
www.bookguild.co.uk
Email: info@bookguild.co.uk
Twitter: @bookguild

Front cover image: *Quercus robur*, English Oak

Typeset in Garamond

Printed and bound in the UK
by TJ International, Padstow, Cornwall

ISBN 978 1 910878 15 6

British Library Cataloguing in Publication Data.
A catalogue record for this book is available from the British Library.

To Anne

ACKNOWLEDGEMENT

I wish to thank my daughter Joanna for her help and assistance in typing up my poems, and for her encouragement.

CONTENTS

WHITE HORSES

I like to go where the strong winds blow
Against the surf of the wild North Sea,
Lifting showers of spray
Back from the surging tide;
Where seabirds stalk the water's edge,
And a gull's cry is a baby's cry
From far away where I cannot go.
O Scarborough, tell me your stories
Of the deep sea, salt and foam,
And I will trade with you
Everything that I know.

As I was walking on Scarborough beach
One Winter's day, when the sky was low,
A great ship left the harbour mouth
And swung into the waves.
It pitched and tossed upon the swell,
And seemed to dance with utter joy
To be at sea again.
O Scarborough, sing me a shanty
Of the deep sea, salt and foam,
And I will play you a hornpipe
To the tunes of long ago.

I dreamed I saw a white horse
That charged across the sea;
Its mane was streaming in the flow,
Its path was symmetry.
And on its back there rode a child
Whose name was known to the clouds above
That came from January.
O Scarborough, sing me a song
Of the deep sea, salt and foam,
And I will give to you
A riddle in a poem

SEA HOLLY

O prickly, elusive eryngium,
So hard to find, there may be none.
The seashore is your natural home,
Above the tidemark, in full sun.
Your bluish leaves, like holly, spiked,
Attract the eye like azurite.
Your flowers like thistles, but powder blue,
Have collared bract and bristles through.
Perhaps on some secluded channel beach
We find you hiding near an upturned boat.
That tap root, deep in dry and pebbly sand,
Seeks out sweet water from far underground.
Living near the ocean's salty spray, who knows
What lies within the aura of your charm.

SKIPPING ON SHROVE TUESDAY

It's Shrove Tuesday,
The East Wind blows,
And Scarborough's up for jumping.
They've closed the road
Along the front,
And strung up flags and bunting.

Down Newborough
And Eastborough
The young 'uns come for skipping;
There's New Steps
And Lifeboat Steps
And lots of pancake flipping.

See two-headed tenpennies
And facial masks
At the gift shop on the corner;
And hot dogs with mustard
At the kiosk
Or burger and onions t' warm yer

At the Crab Stalls there's kippers,
Mussels for dippers,
And lobsters with claws like a vice.
You really should stop
At the Fish and Chip shop,
Where the haddock is good at the price.

At the seafront inn,
A very fine inn,

The revellers make for laughter;
        You can end your day
        Where they begin,
Though the skipping can't come after.

        And it's now they start skipping,
        Though some are near tripping,
In the road on the edge of the crowd.
        The ropes stretch crossways,
        They're raising and dipping,
And the traffic is not allowed.

        As it swings,
        They jump over the rope;
If it all goes wrong then they stop.
        They jump and they skip,
        And sometimes they flip,
When the rope goes down with a flop.

        Young men come out
        To catch the girls,
And pull them in the water.
        The girls run off
        With shrieks and whirls,
And think they didn't ought'er.

        The sea rolls in,
        Snow flurries begin,
And the light fades over the harbour.
        So we'll go our ways
        To the amusement arcades,
And strike a few pennies in Scarborough.

THE SANDMAN

I saw a Sandman
On Scarborough beach,
On a wild March day
By Blackrocks Reach.
His face was grains,
His smile a twist in the tide
That came and went.
I asked him how it came to be,
But his reply was unimaginable.

Great foaming rollers
Sped in past the bar;
Their breaking crests of white water
Tumbled in with thundering roar.
Along the high waves, surfers soared,
Experts in their water sport,
Racing in to shore.

Turning to me, the Sandman
Began to speak of the sea;
Of wind and storm and shipwrecks,
And of things that would come to be.
His eyes were made of seashells,
His nose was lobster red;
And the wind blew through strands of seaweed,
Which grew from the top of his head.

His laugh was that of a wildness
That had never known any control;
Like the plunging waves of the shallows,
Or an Arctic Skua calling below.
He said that he'd seen Lord Nelson,
And the British fleet off Cadiz;
Their sails stretched out to the heavens,
And their ensigns taut in the breeze.

I watched him walk in the water,
And he sang me a strange sea song;
Of sailing ships and shanties,
And of sailors that are now long gone.
Then a cresting wave caught him,
And he disappeared in the sea;
To the sound of a hornpipe and drum,
And the cheers of Nelson's navy.

BENEATH THE WINTER HEDGE

Beneath the slumbering beechwood hedge,
Still in Winter's harsh and leaden grip;
The winnowing wind stirs up dead leaves
That rush against the mossy lawn's straight edge.
Betony beckons here with long curved stems,
Once summery flower'd, now dry and withered up;
Myriad seeds rattle in husks encupped,
That wait upon the seasons for their purple diadems.

Deep down within the fallen litter snowdrops stir,
Advancing their first-foot shoots while yet the year
Is scarcely new, tiny bayonets peeping out
As if to scout the ground about peradventure;
Then swelling up like candle bulbs, white flowers
Appear, unopened yet against cold February's blast;
Until at last their petals part, green-lipped and chaste,
Fluttering in the flurries of snow and frosty air.

Christmas Day 2014

ISABELLA AMALFI

Reaching for the splendour of the sun,
The many-coloured croci open their petals wide;
Banks of purple and white await pollination,
Scattered among fallen stones and plinths beside.

The tumbled ruins on this arid hillside expanse
Lie abandoned, and adopted by the wayside weeds;
Reminder of former glories, echoes of romance,
Which stirs the imagination in rustling laurel leaves.

I saw an early bee amongst the crocus cups,
Alone and solitary, visiting each flower.
Below the swaying cypress trees it flew,
Collecting yellow pollen from Iridaceae.

Next day I found that one lone bee
Had brought a swarm, a host of friends to see
The dazzling brilliance of those croci, spread
Around the ruined temple, where time itself had fled.

I heard the drone of many bees,
Saw square-shaped stones and Juno's ancient temple frieze;
That fleeting glimpse transfixed in sound and sight:
I saw her face in stars of brilliant aconite.

A soldier came with his rifle slung
across his shoulder, an American;
And by his side was an Italian girl
With deep black hair caught up in a curl.

They sat upon a square-shaped stone,
And thinking that they were alone,
Looked at each other with enquiring eyes,
Smiled and kissed beneath blue Roman skies.

Then an armoured column drove through below,
With General Clark, who to Rome would go.
The dust it swirled as the army passed;
All that week it came as the Allies advanced.

The soldier he went off to war,
They parted there in the Cypress grove;
With promises made to meet once more
In the temple ruins, when times improved.

He joined his column as it headed North
From the Alban Hills to the city's edge.
She saw him not from that day forth,
But she kept in her heart their romantic pledge.

Lovers came, but they didn't belong,
She kept to her work in the cafes and bars;
In the hot city streets the war had moved on,
And Italy changed to the Allied cause.

Throughout this time she surely knew
That her American friend was alive and well;
His heart was hers, unchanged and true:
He would return when the war was won.

Two years passed by, with peace restored,
The City of Rome had returned to its trade.
Isabella Amalfi, for such was her name,
Remembered the pact which her soldier had made.

In early Spring she took the road South,
That would bring her back to the Alban hill.
She walked up the steep track that led to the top,
And came to the place she remembered still.

There lay the temple of Juno in ruins,
The stones unmoved, each in its place;
And just as she'd seen them, the croci in bloom,
The cups opened wide with the sun in their face.

She sat upon a square-shaped stone,
And waited there the whole day long;
With thoughts of streets and sounds of Rome,
And listened to the blackcap's song.

O sunny bird of orange trees,
That perches on a canopy,
And sings all day amongst the pleasant leaves:
That I might share your ecstasy.

As yearns the heart for happiness,
So does imagination sometimes invent,
And listening most carefully, intent,
She picked out quiet footsteps from silence.

Quickly, eagerly, the American approached,
Upon the stony track that she had climbed;
Until he reached the temple, where he stopped,
Saw her upon the stone, rushed toward.

Even before they touched, they knew at once
That fate had offered them a second chance.
Taking the pebbly track that led below,
They set off down, without a backward glance.

A passing army jeep took them to Rome,
Where Isabella Amalfi and her American
Were married in S. Costanza church;
In those streets they worked and made their home.

I heard the drone of many bees,
Saw crocus flowers below the waving cypress trees;
That floating scent upon the air which comes at night,
I saw her face in stars of brilliant aconite.

IF VIOLETS COULD SHRINK

Violet, common dog,
Secluded in a Pennine wood;
Clings to shade and damp,
Toadstools and rotten log.
Velvet and blue blooms
Peep through fallen cones,
Seeking residual light
That filters through the canopy.

A trickling stream ran through the wood,
Descending from the high moor's edge.
We crossed the little bridge nearby
Then placing our feet gingerly
Across tussocks of cushioned moss,
Peered into the lichened trees,
Saw tiny wood anemones.

Violets that could shrink no more
Were spread upon the forest floor;
Tiny stems with bluish cups,
Who would know that they were here?
The busy road ran ever by,
But no one stopped nor ventured near.
The tinkling brook meandered through
To Fewston Water down below.

More recently when I passed by,
A chainsaw team was busy there,
Felling swathes of trees like crops,
A cutting edge that starts and stops;
Dead wood laid flat,
Cut into lengths, sawn off.
A few birch trees remained to tell
The sorry story of the dell.

I drove past quickly,
The car climbing the steep road
That twists up snarling bends
Onto Blubberhouses Moor,
Where weathered crags jut out
Like jaws, like clashing rocks,
Pointing to the open sky.
From the summit of the pass
Pendle lay invisible in the haze ahead,
Maybe thirty miles away,
Far down the valley, lost today,
But I knew it was there.

VASE

So romanesque
This rustic vase,
In iridescent
Turquoise glass;
From Vindolanda
Near the wall,
Lapis lazulae
And tall.
Potassium, sand
And soda salt;
Hadrianic
Image caught.
Intangibile
E splendido,
Che oggetto
Di mistero.

HIGHFIELD ROAD

Looking across from Highfield Road
Early on a cold Winter's morning,
I remember seeing Winder covered in fresh snow,
Sparkling in the sun's rays rising.

From the treeline up to the summit,
The hillside was covered in white;
As I walked briskly along the tarmac,
A cold wind began to bite.

Here it was we had our snow fight
That Winter's day so long ago;
Walking out from Winder House gateway,
We were ambushed in the deep snow.

Some boys from school I did not know
Threw snowballs hard across the track.
They had the field, we the roadway,
We walked right into their attack.

I met those young men face to face,
Took a snowball on my head;
Exchanged some words across the fence,
It was their eyes that spoke, not what they said.

Suddenly it dissolved in laughter,
In the cold air we were no longer cold;
Had I sense, I would have asked them,
Who they were, would they have told?

POLYANTHUS

Between two rocks
The Polyanthus grows,
Tucked in a crevice
By the waterfall.
Its dark green leaves
A parasol,
Rest upon the mossy stones
Absorbing light.
Deep down, its crown
Nestles in the overhang,
Keeping shade;
To sprout new shoots
And send down roots
Through niches and cracks
Where moisture clings
To adjacent rocks.
In Spring its flowers
Bloom red and amber,
Peeping from the stones
To catch the sun;
And Summer's heat
Dries out the pods
Whose seeds spill out
Upon the grass below.

BENEATH APPLE TREES

Beneath apple trees in early June
Bluebells flower amongst uncut grass;
Violet-blue for Coronation Day.
Blossom bursts from swelling buds at last.
This year Spring rain saturated the earth,
And cold winds delayed the season, until passed.
So late the lithospermum beds, a dizzy worth,
Display heavenly blue and star, a sport if fast.
Germander speedwell peeps, a paler blue,
Below the steps, if there your eye is cast;
And between stones, field forget-me-not,
Whose turquoise florets should not be overlooked.
Starry chinodoxae spread along the rocky run,
As bright as sapphires in the morning sun.

COLOURED ROCKS

Window sill,
Coloured rocks,
Each within a perspex box;
Some are shiny, others rough,
Bearing signs of igneous birth.
Boxes labelled,
Each to its own;
Geological specimens,
Fired or crystal grown.

Blue and purple: azurite,
Grey from Canada: cobaltite.
Turquoise comes
From Cornwall's mines;
Fuchsite mica, chrome bearing,
From Brazil, shines.
Pyromorphite, Cumbria is
Lead phosphate chlorite;
And cinnabar from Almaden, Spain
Is exotic mercury sulphite.

Cassiterite and sphalerite,
Wolframite and chalcopyrite:
These are all metallic ores;
Some are harmless, others noxious.
There to look at if you but pause,
Considered intellectual boxes.

SPLASH LANE

When April rain falls softly on the ground,
And celandine reveals its yellow flower;
Then would I venture forth upon Splash Lane,
Turning my face into the passing shower.
How often would I walk this pleasant road,
Observing as I went the seasons change.
Splashing in the puddles after rain,
I'd go to see the fields where Corburn flowed.

As fast I'd stride the long way round
Past views familiar to me yet;
Where ran clear water in the ditch,
Grew stitchwort, dead nettle and violet.
And as I walked that winding lane,
I'd look for nests along the hedge;
And if some bird should bolt in fright,
I'd climb right up and search.

Here's the Yellowhammer; I pause to hear him sing
Repeated notes, then one that's not so low.
The sight and sound of southern shores he'll bring,
And make his home in some covert hedgerow.
But secretive and quick to flight is he,
If he should see a movement, he'll be gone.
Then creep along the hedges furtively,
While listening attentively to his song.

Singing thus, suppose the hammer's ring
Upon some metal anvil strikes the note;
The call of distant lands and of the wild
Comes clear across the pastures, but remote.
The Yellowhammer is a travelling bird,
That's never long to stay in any place.
He perches on the blazing gorse in Summer,
Then gypsy-like he's gone without a trace.

And though I live now far away,
I sometimes tread again the old familiar track,
Where once I gleaned for favoured poesy
Those very words that surely draw me back.
Swathes of red campion still adorn the way,
And sprinkled gems of forget-me-not cast blue.
My steps fall brightly in the puddled stray
To Corburn's tinkling brook, and to adieu.

BAUGH FELL

Above Danny Bridge the grassy track extends
Across the wild moor to Muddy Slide,
Redolent feature of the Wilson Run.
Falling sharply there, the path descends
To Hebblethwaite Hall Gill, once Elysium.
Trace the rushing waters up the hill,
Passing jagged cliffs which rise beside;
To climb the testing steepness of Baugh Fell.

On reaching the rim you will then find
A high stone wall to clamber over.
Raise your head above the wall top,
And every sheep grazing on the plateau
Will look across the broad expanse of moor,
See you at once, and stop to stare.
A panoramic view now lies behind you.

It's not wild boars you'll find up here,
Though doubtless they roamed this terrain once;
It's big-horned rams that might appear,
Depending upon the time of year.
The wide open skies are never-ending.
Watch for the elusive, but trusting dotterel,
And cold grey mists, unheralded, descending.

POEM OF THE STONES

Stored in silicon memories, untapped,
The record of these stones must surely
Be able to tell us something of the past,
And of how they came to be settled
Here in the bed of the Corburn.
The larger, rough and deep-scored,
For now Kings of their own domain,
To stand above the crowd,
And peep, curious, over the flow
Of black water rushing past.

The smaller, smooth, submerged,
Close-fitting with rubbed-round edges,
Are favoured by sticklebacks;
Their common fate to be ground down,
Eroded by the swift waters of the brook,
Pebble-dash, then sand.
Perhaps the larger never move,
But shrink imperceptibly,
While the smaller go tumbling down in floods.
If only the stones could speak,
What would they tell us?

Here beneath the larch trees on the hillside,
We stepped across the stones,
My daughters Joanna, Caroline, and I.
Picking the kingstones from their place,
We laid the foundation of an island
In the centre of the stream,
Splitting the strong resistance of the current,
Pitting mass of stone against force of water;
Measuring the flow against the keystone
At the front, where I stood, watching,
Sown in my dreams like the corn.

When I returned in the Spring,
I expected to find no trace of our work;
But I found it still intact, only now,
Filtered through flash floods,
A layer of fine and coarse-grained sand
Had been deposited like grit in the stones' teeth;
And a colony of pioneer grass
Had settled over that.
Around the edges, its seeds waterborne,
Brooklime had taken root,
Gripped tight by the teeth
In the strong flow of rushing water;
Its bright blue flowers, like little gems,
Were anchored fast on straggly stems.

From the rushes across the marshy ground
A snipe, alarmed, flew low and fast
Down towards Stagshaw bridge below,
Uttering its piercing, piping cry;
An upland and a childhood sound
That I remember still.

It seemed surprising that the island
Had not been spoiled nor washed away,
But had become a natural feature of the stream.
Nature, it seemed, had endorsed
Our primitive idea, and perhaps we also
Were to be considered primitive by instinct,
For putting it there in the first place.

THE WILD GARDEN

I knew a garden, wild and free,
Where wild flowers shared their pedigree
With Marguerite and Columbine;
Where Crocus grew with Celandine,
And room was made for all that came,
For I knew every one by name.

The grass grew tall and sent up sprays
Of seed that swayed in the passing wind;
Blue Californian Hyacinths,
Nasturtia winding round a plinth
Of Roman rocks set in a wall;
Orange trumpets free-for-all.

In borders edged with London Pride,
Foxglove and Lupin stood side by side;
Sweet William, Mint and pale Harebell,
Ladybird and Tortoiseshell;
And in a secret place I found
Bindweed and Honeysuckle intertwined.

26

From my slopes I sent down seed
That found good ground and was not weed:
Willow Herb and Thistledown,
Yellow Ragwort and Dandelion.
In amongst the flowers they fell;
Where they were I could not tell.

The wind and rain were friends to me,
Like the garden, they were wild and free.
I drank the rain whenever it fell,
And the wind drew whispers through my hair
Which turned to gold as the days grew long,
And I was there for everyone.

EARLY JUNE

The third of June:
The TV happily said that
Today's the first day of Summer;
It lives up to its name,
Growing hotter hour by hour.
A clear blue sky stirs wispy winds,
And in the distance a small white cloud
Floats like lilac scent upon the air.
Unseen, wild birds
Sing in the leafy garden trees.
Apple blossom is on the bough;
Plum has pollinated, tiny fruits now:
Lithospermum heavenly blue,
Hebe Pinguifolia bunched white,
And creeping Pink Phlox across the top
Of that large stone upon the wall, all
Trailing shoots which flower and fall.
Across orange courts at Roland Garros
The Paris crowds watch tennis matches.
A bottle of red Bordeaux mulls my thought:
Days long and hot, nights are short.

THE WILD PEAR TREE

How refined and independent is Pyrus Communis,
That pear which seeks to grow in wilderness.
You prosper in dry southern plains;
Untouched by time, your origin remains.
That pyramidal form and measured height
Are close to conical, and much admired.
In Spring your blossoms are brilliant white,
In clustered corymbs that scent the night;
But Autumn's promise of fruit may disappoint:
Too harsh to eat, though try you might.
Walking across the flat Cornish fields,
I came upon this solitary tree;
How strange and wonderful to find it there,
A glory of the plains: the pure Wild Pear.

CAYTON BAY

It was steep, descending,
And we took care not to slip
Where loose sand lay,
Treacherous on the incline.
The path fell away at the foot,
Where winter storms
Had undermined the clay.
Picking our way down wooden steps,
We ran fast across the empty beach,
Choosing a sheltered site
To place our baggage down.
Overhead black and white clouds
Sailed seaward like wild geese
On a fresh blustery day.
The sea roared untamed,
Tumbling in to shore restlessly.

Tossing aside odd clothes,
We raced barefoot
Down Cayton Beach
Along the sand, until, breathless,
We reached the southern edge.
Grey cliffs stood
Monumental and immense
To our side and front;
Seagulls screamed down.
Amongst the flotsam
We found a fisherman's float,
Made of polystyrene;
And, throwing it into the sea,
Hurled pebbles after it.
Returning, we dashed through the spray,
Jumping into cresting waves,
Gasping at the cold shock of it.

When I emerged,
I ran to the wartime pillbox to change,
Taking possession just in time,
As rain fell suddenly and heavily.
Jeans clung damp and uncomfortable.
My children joined me inside.
Peering through gunslits,
We talked of pirates,
Smugglers and Eccles cakes,
And wished the rain would stop.

THE HAWTHORN TREE

I found an old hawthorn on a Yorkshire hill
Whose branches swept the sea winds for their stories,
Twisting and screwing them into its gnarled trunk
To catch the thread of their yarn in its eye.
To windward yards weathered constant gales,
Which buffeted the tree in its exposed position,
So that it gripped the slope and held fast
With long surface roots embedded in the clay.
In Summer, cows would languish in its shade,
Swatting flies, and snorting in the heat.
A carrion crow built a nest in the mizzen,
And a little girl skipped and flew her kite.
The tree blossomed pink and white in May,
And it sang to the wind on the Roman Way.

THE OLD WINDMILL

Down Wykeham Street, the road points to the mill.
Graffiti daubed on walls beside the old railway line
Depict fantastic faces and colourful artwork.
The marshalling yard and its turntable have gone,
Replaced by play areas, a supermarket and parking.
Over the humpback bridge the children come,
Shouldering satchels on their way to school.
They scream and dash across the crowded school yard,
Hop, skip and jump over the painted numbers.

Down Roscoe Street a welding torch flickers
Inside the wrought-iron workshop across the road.
Garages for car repairs, hair salon and beauty clinic
Stand among terraces of Victorian houses:
Rustic bricks in vermilion and faded red,
With roofs of lilac slate, purple when wet.
Quaint chimney stacks are topped with clay pots,
Tall or stout, toothed rim or flat,
Others with lids to keep the rain out.

Above the chimneys stands the old windmill;
With white sails static, it's now an hotel.
The weathered brick shell tapers, pencil drawn
To a dome like an inverted force-cup.
Small high windows give good light, and wide views
Over roofs, chimneys, school and bridge.
Walking down the hump on Wykeham Street,
The mill sinks slowly beneath the chimney pots,
Until at last it disappears below.

PALM COURT

Radio orchestra,
Closed doors;
Reading room,
Applause.
Light music,
Good books;
Undercover
She looks.
Chopin's Nocturnes,
Brendel plays;
I leave early,
She stays.

PENNY WISE

I sometimes wonder at the saying
'Seek and you will find';
For very much would depend upon
What you had in mind.

As official in charge of envelopes
For the local parish church,
It had never been my intention
To carry out a search.

The weekly transformation
From secrecy to bank
Was achieved with such discretion,
That I never knew whom to thank.

I remember opening an envelope
Inside of which I found
A solitary penny
Which should have been a pound.

The most that could be said was that
As an amount it was certainly round;
But in view of the donor's intentions,
To God it was a pound.

Another proverb I recall
Begins with 'Penny Wise';
But if a pound is foolish,
Which would you advise?

THE BLACKTHORN THICKET

When March's gusty winds and frosts still grip the land,
Then blackthorn sparks the hedgerows and surrounds
With pure white blossoms, starry-flecked and bright,
Which catch the eye where all else is dull to sight.
Prunus Spinosa is that many-branched shrub
That forms dense thickets in which the fox may hide;
Whose buds hold back within their sheltering sheaves
'Til Spring is here, and then produce their leaves.
I know a blackthorn thicket, close to a woody edge,
Where Corburn rushes past, by butterbur and sedge;
There it was the long-tailed tit did make its domed nest,
Woven between sharp twigs, with moss and feathers dressed.
Long gone were they before the Autumn rain,
When green leaves fell away, and Winter came.
But blackthorn surprised us all with purple sloes,
That fruit of dusky bloom which on Spinosa grows,
Beside the Stagshaw bridge, where no one goes.

THE RAINMAN

O let me lie on springy grass,
Fortescue and sphagnum moss;
The dampness in it will soon pass,
Cuckoo spit and candy floss.

I fix my eyes on passing clouds:
A sailing ship to foreign lands.
The warm wind spurs the billowing shrouds,
And at its helm the Rainman stands.

Above the hill his colours come,
Pastel grey and bespoke dun;
Columns of blue with pipe and drum,
Scissors flash before the sun.

Where the wind blows he will go,
Over the surf to far Cathay.
Where he's now I would not know,
But he'll be back another day.

SPINNING CHANCE

With sleight of hand the bowler's wrist
Is cleverly concealed in twist;
Stitch and seam across red leather,
Swing and googly work together.
Graphic-flighted through the air,
Penny accurate on pitch;
Landing where there's rough and wear,
Breaking 'off' or 'leg', but which?
Batsman blocks if he can see it,
Yorkers need a lucky glance;
Bouncing through to hit the wicket,
Bowler stands an even chance.
Off and on, they just might make it,
But can their alter ego take it?

THE NOT-CRICKET MATCH

The Cricket Match was under way,
Somewhere near Leeds, on a Summer's day.
A Lancashire team were in to bat,
And a Yorkshire team fielded,
The White Rose, 'How's that?'
The score was twenty-eight for five,
When Number Seven struck an off drive.
Just short of boundary he was caught,
And he went in the book for nought.
From the pavilion came Number Eight,
Ambling on with padded gait.

'Red Rose or White?' the bowler asked,
'Red, of course,' was the reply.
The bowler sprinted to the crease,
And loosed a ball with practised ease.
Through the air its flight was slow,
Landing penny-accurate below
The bat, which didn't even snick it;
It flicked a bail right off the wicket.

'A Yorker, that,' the bowler said,
Yorkshire born and Yorkshire bred;
And then addressed the new arrival,
Who seemed more skilful at survival.
'Middle and Leg,' the batsman said,
The umpire lined it to the peg,
And up the bowler came once more,
To settle yet another score.

But scoring of another kind
Was what the batsman had in mind.
He struck the ball through Middle-on,
It nearly cleared the field in one.
Bouncing far, it gathered pace,
As Middle-on began to chase.
Not quite six, a splendid four,
It ended on a dented door.

'That's my car, you stupid beggar,'
The bowler said with obvious vigour.
'Why don't you try your hand at Rugger?'
Then 'Red Rose or White?' he asked again,
The googly in his humour masked.
'Red, of course,' was the reply;
'You want a fight, just come and try.
We all come from Burnley Town,
And we are going to knock you down.'

'Walk off,' the bowler then replied,
As all his mates ran to his side,
'You're in Yorkshire now, you red-rosed prat,
I'll fix your nose, so just take that!'
And saying this, they all set to,
With feet and fists and headbutts too.
Struggling and pushing across the pitch,
White versus white, but which was which?

The umpire put the bails in pocket,
I heard him say, 'Now just you knock it.
I've never seen owt like this before,
I'll declare match void if there's any more!'
There was no way they would agree,
So up they got and went for tea.
A notice went up on the board,
'Match Abandoned – Dispute Tied'.

DOUBLE AGENT MI5

Double agent with an inside view,
Insider dealer, I thought like you
That the best way of dealing
With the opposite side,
Is to climb right inside them
And look outside.

Double agent with buzzwords to match,
You were watching their secret dispatch.
Your information
When added to mine,
Will turn the clock movement
Backwards in time.

Double agent, you slipped right in,
They didn't see the slightest thing;
But your sleight of hand
Shows a flair for design,
To draw out extremists
And stop them in time.

VICTORIA PLUM

Victoria Plum, O purple one,
That fruit which connoisseurs have doted on;
Your honey'd taste is well disguised,
Each year's first plum a new surprise.
As bitter is the immature,
No wasp nor other will go near;
But changed to deeper red and soft,
One gentle turn will twist it off.
Victoria Plum, ascendant one,
Growing next to Lord Lambourne;
You give a really good impression,
Especially to the head, in Autumn.
No bird has found your secret yet;
Then scented blossoms from late frost protect.

LIKE AN AZALEA

Like an azalea
I found you,
Deep in the foothills
Of my foreign mountain mind;
Steep was the escarpment
That I encountered,
Oh, the rocks that I climbed!
Searching for magnolia
Or aromatic buddleia,
I struck pitons
In remote regions,
Discovered what I came to find.

With such hopes
And ambitions I had come,
Collecting for English Summers
In subtropical rain;
And having once found you,
I could not hope for more,
It would never be the same.
Deftly I took the seed
To raise in sheltered glass;
Then, stepping like a tiger,
I turned for home again.

WILD ROSE

Here's to beauty! both in form and scent:
To the Wild Rose that in England has kept
Sentinel upon the leas and hedgerows
Of this our native land. Raise your glasses
To that inestimable one, whose pink
And white sweet-scented blooms dress our greens
With bolder hues, peeping out
In Summer's heat from vantage points between,
To meet the traveller's curious passing gaze.

The Dog Rose is its bookish name,
(Rosa Canina) though few speak thus of it,
But maybe for its roughish bark, as brier.
Rather be it that English Rose, depicting
Some fair country girl of whom one might enquire.
O Wild Rose, that adorns our fields and lanes,
Becoming those scarlet fruits we know as hips,
Which once as children we collected by the pound
To trade for pennies in some village shop.

Once Tudor Rose, now England's National Flower,
Its curving thorns resist all those
Who would by intrusion push on through.
Beautiful to those who would admire:
Wild Rose of England, here's to you!

THE ITALIAN GARDENS, ESPLANADE

I strolled down sunlit paths above the sea,
Admiring the sweep of Scarborough's Esplanade.
Freehold flats and hotels lined the hill,
Looking out upon the broad South Bay,
Past borders of showy bedding plants in bloom.
Along the rim of the South Cliff, painted black,
A railing led the way along the track,
To where a stunted Scotch Pine, swept by sea winds,
Reached low across the path, which I admired.

Opposite Holbeck Road, a putting green
Gives panoramic views both North and South;
There's no one playing yet, they're all inside.
An elegant clock tower, time correct, stands clear,
Its four faces high, where they can be seen;
Open below, with marble floors, a shelter from rain;
Above, a cupola and weather vane.
Across the road, with extensive well-cut lawns,
Is Shuttleworth Gardens, open all year.

Below the Esplanade, through trees and shrubs,
The path descends the gradient in curves,
Reaching a sylvan grove set out to plan:
The Italian Gardens, suggestive of another age.
Here the borders, planted out in beds,
Await the occasional visitor's curious gaze.
A pond, four-leafed, flag iris filled,
Contains a statue on a broad stone plinth:
Mercury, the messenger god of Rome.

He leaps across the water in wingéd pose.
Bright sun, reflecting from the shimmering pond,
Glances across the statue to create
Rippling effects of light upon its face.
Beyond, Doric columns form a colonnade,
With mysterious shadows merging into shade;
For days are short here below the cliff,
Where sun is sparse, though light may well persist,
And heavy perfumed scents pervade the air.

I rested on a low wall, and presently
Came shy creatures, enquiring after food,
Eyes bright, trusting, but alert:
A squirrel and a pigeon, but none I had.
That poets come to write is no surprise;
Inspiration comes in many a guise,
Maybe through the genius of this place.
A thunderstorm approached, violent and dark;
Climb I must, if wet, the steep way home.

SUMMER DAYS

On this hot July day, brambles were in bloom,
Encouraged by Mother Sun, opening their petals wide
Unto a cloudless sky and soaring Red Kite.
Throughout the bramble patch, myriad bees descended
On heavy-scented flowers, prickly and white,
Set in tight bunches beyond my garden fence,
Where none can go but cows, discreetly out of sight.
Then, darting to and fro, a Ringlet butterfly
Emerged from tall standing grass to alight
Upon a bramble flower, then moving on,
Flitting along each bush in erratic flight.
At dusk that blazing orb will set beyond Suffield hill,
And the fierce heat of Summer days
Will fall into the purple night.

BRAMBLE BUSH

Oh how pale and white are the petals
Of the prickly bramble bush;
That might please the eye of a beholder,
Though I believe there be nonesuch.

But the bee comes from its garden
To search for pollen there;
And the Ringlet, darting back and forth,
With favoured knapweed might compare.

In forest glade and thicket,
Wherever startled pheasants rise;
Down woodland rides and steep hillsides,
Withal the tangled bramble thrives.

Though its flowers be pure white in Summer,
And their scent attracts the bee;
Tis the purple fruit of Autumn
That's the glory of the Blackberry.

THE
EXPERIMENTAL
GARDEN

Experimental
Wildflower plot;
Vegetable garden,
Convenient spot.
Rake it over,
Sift the soil;
Sprinkle seeds,
Wait a while.
In April and May
Fall seasonal showers;
June and July,
Wait for flowers.
August comes,
The sun so hot;
Blue cornflowers
Come bursting out;
Corncockle, larkspur,
Forget-me-not;
Pheasant's eye, pansy,
What a lot.
I wait to see
White campion,
Corn marigold:
Yellow sunshine.

Buttercups and poppies
From cornfields past,
Here they have
A home at last.
Visited by bumble bee,
Who will match their rarity!
Wayside flowers
And meadow blooms;
The experimental plot
With gems festooned.
Left in Autumn,
The seed will fall;
Winter comes
And covers all.
In Spring their seeds
Will come again,
Awaiting sun
And catalyst rain.

CORNELIAN BAY

Cornelian Bay, romantic in its solitude,
Down steep inclines, is hard to reach.
Slippery slopes and jagged rocks impede
The wanderer's access to this lonely beach,
Where silence and sea creep stealthily upon each
Successive tidemark of torn seaweed.

Rounded pebbles washed ashore in storms
Cover the curving beach, their many tones
Of colour blend: heliotrope, dun and grey,
Thrown into heaps, ribbons of sand among stones.
Here are many seashells: whelks and limpet cones;
Periwinkles tossed about, amidst the flying spray.

Undiscovered in the shingle, cornelians lie,
Bright and shiny orange, glinting in sunshine,
Which falls aslant the sloping scree and sand.
A wartime pillbox looks both ways along the waterline,
And beyond there lies uprooted a sunbleached Scotch Pine,
Washed in from some far shore or distant land.

It was here we came one glorious Summer's day,
Our eyes bright with adventure, my daughters and I.
Advancing across the pebbles, we climbed the fort's rampart
Placing feet in well-cut steps which no one found too high.
From across the rocks there arose the sandpiper's piercing cry,
Reminding me of upland streams, half a year apart.

Beyond the pillbox we walked on for half a mile,
Pausing then to camp upon that desolate shore.
We built a fire with driftwood and anything that burned,
Searching in the wooded brakes for more.
Around our fire we listened to the ocean's adjacent roar,
Toasted bread on twiggy prongs and waited while it turned.

A spark flew out and landed on our tartan rug,
Which singed a hole that remains a hole today:
The same rug my mother bought from Otterburn Mill.
The fire grew bright, and cheered us where we lay,
Watching the sea shapes, passing time away,
Talking and laughing, which I remember still.

The smouldering embers of our fire dwindled low,
As, gathering up our possessions, we rose to go.
I remember now the way it was:
The sea, the pebbled shore, the burnt-out final glow.
We struck inland through scrub and sand because
The fading light and time had made it so.

The wild seascape and shoreline lay below,
As on we went, climbing the steep cliff face;
Pulling ourselves up, clinging to stems and roots until
Eventually we reached the top, an edgy place,
Where erosion crumbles the lip without a trace
Of warning; here we stood and looked downhill.

We heard the curlew's haunting cry
That called across Cornelian Bay,
And turned for home along the Coastal Path,
Whose name we saw upon a sign, 'The Cleveland Way'.
Down this we wandered, finding a turquoise towel
Abandoned in a puddle, from New York City.

THE OLD OAK TREE

Hail to the mighty robust Oak,
Our longest-lived and largest native tree,
Whose boughs stretch out with rugged strength
To hold the weight of gnarled and twisted limbs!
The bark upon its massive trunk is deeply lined
And scored with jagged fissures throughout its length.
Dark green leaves, ovate and roundly lobed
Bear auricles at each leaf's base, which, understood,
Would help identify the species: Quercus Robur.
In Autumn, mature acorns fall to earth,
Fodder for wild hogs, red squirrels and the like;
And some few germinate, to strike new seedlings
Upon the forest floor or countryside.
Who has not heard of oak apples? Maybe not seen
Those wasp and spangle galls, small hard mysteries
Which attach themselves to twiglets or to leaves.
Beneath the tree's shade on halcyon Summer days,
Come courting couples to while away the hours;
Doubtless valued then, and remembered in years to come.

SEPTEMBER SUN

September sun;
The dry cracked earth
Lies open-mouthed,
Waiting for rain.
Prolonged drought
Has scorched out
The top spit,
Spade deep,
Which crumbles to dust
At the pronged thrust
Of a garden fork.
Lift, turn,
Disturb worm,
Wriggle back.
Scatter black
Bonfire ash
With leafmould,
On flattened patch
Where ridged rows stood
Back to back.
Baked potatoes,
Clean-skinned,
Dusted off,
Riddled and stored;
Deplored small size,
Peas eyes,
Surprised
At sundown,
New moon,
Indoors too soon.

ARGYRANTHEMUM

Argyranthemum
In old clay pot;
Blooms, Paris daisy,
Red with yellow spot.
Terracotta,
Umber urn;
Warm exterior,
Likes the sun.
Flowers and fruit
To decorate;
Full to brim,
A heavyweight.
Water compost
Every day;
Remove at night
And hide away.
Cuttings cut
From off the stem
Will produce
A little gem.
A plethora
Of flowers to come;
Marguerite
Mediterranean.

CRUSADE

Now Holy England lies covered in snow;
A white altar cloth has been newly laid
Across forests, hilltops and patched fields below,
To soften the tread of the distant crusade.

Oh soldier, soldier, where have you gone?
Your house is cold and your lover's heart torn.
What dangers await you in the days to come,
Amongst the dust devils of Desert Storm?

A silver plate and a crucifix;
Sacraments we can understand.
Icicles bright as candlesticks,
And a cross of twigs for the frozen land.

The psalmist wrote of Midian wars,
Of violent men that all might fear;
Where now the mighty lion roars,
The wingéd beast will reappear.

THE HARVEST

Oh I wish I could see the cornfields
From days of long ago,
When poppies spread wide in a scarlet tide,
And corncockles peeped above the crop
To see how high and when to stop;
When thistles were yellow and sow
 At the edge of the waving corn.
I wish I could see the scattered blue
Of dazzling cornflowers, fit for show.

Oh I wish I could watch the reapers
As they toiled away in a line,
With their scythes sweeping stalk to stubble,
To bring home the harvest in time.
When women and children gathered the straw
To tie into sheaves of three or four,
And stack them in stooks for Winter store.
I wish I had been there to see the corn
When they'd finished at last all tired and worn.

Oh I wish I could see them when the dancing began,
With the work all done and the harvest in.
The fiddlers would play to a merry crowd,
And the young would dance and sing out loud.
The fire burned bright and faces shone,
And all that work might mean was gone.
Some lay and slept, close to the fire,
And I took me home with a pretty girl,
A tankard of beer, and my head in a whirl.

HARVEST FESTIVAL

High Summer dipped into Autumn
With a flourish of mellow days.
At church it was Harvest Festival,
Children brought gifts of fruit and vegetables,
And laid them on the steps below the altar;
Their faces shone like McIntosh Reds.
At home I harvested too,
Clean dry potatoes only needed dusting,
Yielding up easily from the crumbling earth,
In which no moisture remained.
I walked across the empty plot,
And threw woodash and leafmould
Over the flattened ridges.
A robin flew from a nearby fence,
And hopped deftly through the scattered litter,
Looking for seeds and grubs,
While I leaned on my spade to watch.
Two steps to the left, then two to the right,
Swing around in a figure of eight.
I thought of the harvest dance that night,
And went indoors to change.

OCTOBER

Goldfinches twitter excitedly
In the red-berried hawthorn bush
That stands on the seaview hill.
Blackbirds peck at mature red apples
From the top of Laxton's Fortune;
Dislodged, they fall, reserved by holes,
To join windfalls awaiting fruit bowls.
A pale sun glances obliquely across lime trees,
Highlighting violet in Michaelmas daisies.
Gladiolus, showy, so late in the year,
Flowers bottom to top, reversed in a way.
Turning October's dry, dusty soil, I found
Crocus bulbs awake, but not yet dressed.
The garden now waits, as for an unexpected guest.

PENNY BLACK LANE

Penny Black Lane is a pseudonym
For Trafalgar Street West: the road's the same.
The first is a nickname the locals use;
It's really a corruption, a verbal misuse.
Two centuries ago it was Penn's Back Lane;
If you alter two letters, the riddle's plain.
To those that don't know it, they'll never guess,
Though they keep on trying nevertheless.
But Trafalgar Street West is a name they all know,
The Trafalgar pub's on it, and the Council depot.
So remember the enigma of Penny Black Lane:
It's not in the stamp, but it is in the name.

NOVEMBER SONNET

November's cold blustery squall
Blows in from the North with rain.
The young lime in the lane outside
Rustles change and sheds leaves;
Dull yellow remnants scatter and fall.
Bare twigs sweep patterns in the sky.
Wild geese rush past in ragged formation,
Flying South on the edge of the storm,
Seeking refuge on some grassy coastal plain.
Dull red streetlights brighten into orange.
The chimney stack over the road
Sends out a horizontal trail of smoke.
Here come the children home from school;
Laughing and shouting, they splash in each pool.

BERRIES

Bunches of bright red berries
Beckoned just out of reach
At the top of the old holly tree.
Standing on a wobbly fence
On the third Sunday of Advent,
I reached up where others could not.
The west wind buffeted me
As I stood on the topmost rail,
Clinging precariously to a handy twig,
And cut where the berries were thick.
Sprigs of sea green holly fell to earth.
Looking down I saw a child
Whose face was bright with excitement;
Who picked up the twigs,
And put them in bunches neatly away,
To place on pictures for Christmas Day.

Taken from an actual event near Low Fell. The child was my daughter. –
G.T.

BEECH GROVE IN WINTER

Seldom is Fagus Sylvatica more evocative
Than on a wild and blustery Winter's day,
When its topmost twigs sweep a cold grey sky,
And the Beech Grove sighs as the branches sway.
Around lie mossy tussocks, wondrous of age;
        Untroubled, they slumber on,
        Cushions green as sage.
In amongst the beech mast, chaffinches peck at nuts,
        While underground and hidden,
        Fungi form intricate networks.

I sheltered next to the bole of an old and weathered tree,
Mighty in its girth, its bark was grey and coarse.
Looking up, I saw initials carved in deep,
And a piercéd heart with love that will not sleep.
        I thought then of lovers,
        And the north wind did moan.
I picked up my bag of fallen leaves,
And took the long lane home.

I walked up the Downs on a Winter's day,
The wind blew hard, my breath was swept away.
Across the hard shoulder of a limestone rise,
I came on the Beech Grove, and heard its sighs.
Oh, the snow it fell in flurries at first,
Then the air blew cold in wuthering gusts;
And I sheltered there in the grove of beech,
The snow grew thick over tussock and leaf.

A chaffinch came down and hopped all around,
Looking for nuts in the beech tree stand.
I thought of the snow and the little foot tracks,
Of the lover's heart won and my firewood sacks.
Then I took the way home to tend my fire,
Away from the gale and the cold entire;
Back to a hearth in a stone fireplace,
And the wind blew hard in my face,
So, I took to my poems and went home.

THE DOLPHIN

I lay on the beach at Cayton Bay,
  The sun felt hot
  On the sand where I lay.
I looked to my left and I looked to my right,
  And only a shaker
  Of people were out.

  Chorus Hey ho for Cayton Bay,
  And the sun felt hot
  On the sand all day

I went to swim in the wild North Sea,
  The waves were big,
  And they buffeted me;
I swam right out as far as I could go,
  I swam back in,
  But I couldn't get back.

  Chorus Hey ho for Cayton Bay,
  And the sun felt hot
  On the sand all day.

A dolphin came and swam below,
  It raised me up
  And I didn't say no;
It took me to shore with a swish of its tail,
  And it left me there;
  I was pleased to go.

Chorus Hey ho for Cayton Bay,
And the sun felt hot
On the sand all day

I stood on the beach and I looked around,
    The dolphin came close
    To the edge of the sand.
It leaped in the air and it smiled at me,
    It did a full turn,
    Then it swam away.

Chorus Hey ho for Cayton Bay,
The sun felt hot
On the sand where I lay;
I looked to my left and I looked to my right,
    There was no one left,
    There was no one in sight.

FISHING IN THE RIVER TYNE AT CORBRIDGE

I picked my way along the cinder path with care,
Equipped, as goes the eager fisherman, for sport:
A jaunty hat upon my head, my steps in waders caught,
I felt those curtained eyes behind me stare.
It was my wish to fish the evening rise,
So, gripping rod and line, I took the stony track
That led past Coulson's farmyard with its old haystack,
To reach the grassy banks of River Tyne.

The River Tyne at Corbridge, swift and broad,
Is two hundred yards from bank to bank;
Its bed is strewn with pebbles, the edges raised and rank,
With somewhere here a long-forgotten ford.
I walked on up the riverbank to where
The path began to crumble, sandy and steep,
Disappearing into waters black and deep.
A notice here read 'Water 18 feet, Beware'.

Further up the river path I stood,
Looking for a certain place I knew;
Where stunted, sprawling orange willows grew,
Which lined the edge, downswept by flood.
Here there was a gap: I struggled through,
Holding back the willows, sprung and overgrown;
Then wading out, I reached a large flat stone,
Standing clear above the River Tyne.

August's sun was sinking into the western sky,
Its image reflected in waters bright
With orange flame, dancing as if alight.
Standing on the stone, I attached a March Brown fly,
And waxed the line to float: fishing dry,
I drew my line right back, to cast across the flow,
But it got caught upon a bush behind, a willow,
Growing on the banks of River Tyne.

Ignoring the sarcasms of a passing crow,
I retrieved my line, and casting out
With Greenwell's Glory, caught a trout:
Large and fat, I let it go.
I tried again in fading light,
Across the current where eddies twist;
Enveloped then by river mist
Which swirled across the Tyne.

The river's serenity was all around,
It mattered not what fish were caught;
The thought arose that in general, sport
Was achieved by taking part. Hardly a sound
Stirred the still evening's rise.
Out there small trout and dace were rising,
Making circles, appetizing, lapping
Quietly against the muddy riverbank.

When almost dark, I rose myself to go,
With thoughts of trout and sauerkraut;
And much besides to please the palate,
But chance of fish and chips, zero.
Looking down the stream, I saw the bridge below,
Its wide arches etched in fading gloam,
And turned into the lane that took me home.
'Did you catch anything?' they asked: I said 'No.'

THE DUCHESS OF MILAN

There grows a Lily of the Field,*
Where no one goes but I;
Deep in the fields of Lombardy,
Where poplars wave and sigh.

My lady came a-looking,
Amongst the rank long grass;
Searching in the rushes,
For what? I could not guess.

I wandered by the riverside,
Near where the Lily grew;
I wished to gaze upon it,
If it was there to view.

My eyes beheld the lady,
As she reached down in the grass;
She plucked the Lutein Lily,
And was gone with it, alas!

It was no good to follow,
Her coach and horses stood
Waiting by the roadside,
To take her where she would.

The coach was painted black and gold,
A coat of arms upon the door;
Around it armed retainers stood,
The colours of Milan they wore.

She reached the coach and stepped inside,
She placed the Lily in a vase;
Multi-coloured, of expensive glass,
It qualified the gift perchance.

My lady was yet very young,
A Princess of the City State;
Newly married to Ludovico Sforza,
The Regent of Milan.

Her name was Beatrice D'Este,
From Ferrara she had come;
To learn the tricks of politics
Within her situation.

Inside the coach her mother sat,
Attired as for a journey long:
The Duchess of Ferrara;
Their retinue a thousand strong.

Sforza had sent his wife to Venice,
To meet the Doge on his behalf;
Not doubting her, that she was able,
The girl was full of life and shrewd.

They journeyed on through country roads,
Until they reached the River Po;
Where the state barge of Ferrara
Would take them where they wished to go.

Arrived at Venice, they met the Doge,
Attending him at council in his palace;
Where first the Duchess, then Beatrice herself
Thanked them all and explained Milan's purpose,

And then she took the fine glass vase,
Colours bright, as she was able:
The Lutein Lily set in water,
Fresh and fragrant, upon the table.

Addressing the Doge, she said she'd picked it
To give to him when she arrived:
The yellow Lily with golden markings,
More than Solomon in all his attire.**

The Doge stood up and took the vase
And Lutein Lily in his hand;
Beheld its beauty at a glance,
Wise as Solomon, could understand.

He said that though the flower would fade,
The memory of that moment stayed;
As also the beauty of the Princess herself;
That he would value the acquaintance made.

Two years passed by, and then in Autumn
I wandered by the riverside;
Near where the Lily of the Field had grown,
Grass and rushes grew thick beside.

And then I saw its golden glow,
The Lutein Lily which flowers late,
To grace the leas and waving grass,
But only I had come to view.

Not so, for there the coach had stopped,
And down the meadows Beatrice D'Este
Had come to find her flower again,
To pick and take it at its best.

More so, for now she was Duchess herself,
The Duchess of Milan, no less.
Her husband Sforza was the Duke;
Her clothes and jewels did impress.

I stopped and asked her what she wished;
She looked at me and then she smiled:
And then she laughed and danced around,
Said she looked for a Lily wild.

'Ah so,' I said, 'You come again,
To pick the Lily of the Field.'
She seemed surprised, and then replied,
'Not so, for I can see it's yours.'

*Sternbergia Lutea, or Winter Daffodil. Lutein is a yellow pigment.

**St. Matthew 7: 28–29

THE YELLOW GORSE

So full of colour are those hillsides and heaths
That are painted with splashes of flowering gorse;
So thick and spiny, and always most thorny,
But sprinkled throughout with deep yellow blooms.
Ulex Europaeus, its cover so copious,
Can be used as windbreaks and hedges;
Appearing in meadows, on clifftops and ledges,
Its prickly presence will not always please.
But wild birds do like it, will nest in its thicket,
And yellowhammers blend with its flowers in May.
But try to remove it, bulldoze or dig it,
And you'll find that it simply won't go away.
It sprouts out new branches and grows ever thicker,
With more yellow flowers to brighten the day.

JUST ONCE

We walked along the river path East.
The morning sun filtered through a canopy
Of woodland trees; an April sun
Created dappled patterns on the ground.
The River Tyne flowed swiftly past.
A fisherman, thigh-deep in waders,
Stood well out from the bank,
Casting upstream in the strong current.
We went to see the sand martins further down,
Nesting high above the steep sandy slope,
Their tunnels visible, inaccessible,
In a vertical wall of compacted sand.
Martins screamed excitedly
As they dived and weaved in the air.

Then we turned our attention
To the old derelict footbridge
That led across the Tyne.
Long since disused and lacking repair,
The walkway was made of short planks
Arranged crossways, the length of the bridge.
We took it in turns to cross;
To refuse was to lose face.

I walked slowly on, apprehensively,
Hardly daring to look down
Through gaping gaps of missing planks,
The river rushing madly past,
Dark and fast, thirty feet below,
Its stony bed clearly visible,
While the bridge swayed back and forth.
I thought of rotten wood,
Breaking planks, the plunge;
And edged my way slowly across,
Clinging to the handrail,
Seeking the safety that beckoned beyond.

We all made it, and walked back
To Corbridge along the far bank,
Through grounds I hadn't seen before.
I thought 'Just Once'
This risk had paid off,
An extreme sport,
But we never did it again.

BUTTERFLIES

Amongst woody glades and dappled shades
And in full sunshine, wander I;
What keeps the elusive butterfly?
Which species will I see today?

Moving slowly, I see them flit
From buddleia bush to fancied flower;
Guided by scent, nectar intent,
Content with sun nor sheltered bower.

Here we see peacock from August's hatch,
Big-winged, with painted eyes;
And tortoiseshell with bars to match
The very backdrop where it flies.

Large and small whites seek out brassicae
To lay their eggs 'neath cabbage leaf;
Hatching into caterpillars, unpopular,
Which eat large holes and mischief weave.

Red admiral is still absent,
I like to see its bright cocked hat;
But ringlet came in July's hot vent,
Wings with rings on dark chocolate.

Speckled Wood prefers leafy cover,
Its blackish wings picked out with yellow;
Between the fruit trees see it flutter:
Genus is Pararge Aegeria.

I look to find the common blue,
Brimstone, or the orange-tip;
On cuckoo flower or feverfew,
But none I see, nor chance let slip.

TYNE ESTUARY

O estuarine pool, where waters flow
Through murky depths by Jarrow Slake;
Where dredgers sift the silty shallows,
And rafts of flotsam float forth and back.
Here the River Tyne comes down
Through tidal reaches to meet the sea;
Past old red Groyne, whose light is gone,
And long stone piers pointing easterly.

Here are seen leviathans,
Giant ships that dwarf the shore;
And round the point, half-marathon,
The finish of the Great North Run.
Upon the south shore, near the pier,
There stands a fairground and arcade;
Sounds electronic with music on it
Drift across the esplanade.

Up the river, a ferry landing
Is conveniently placed to cross the Tyne;
On the staging, expectant, standing,
A trickle of people wait in line.
We joined the queue and passed on through,
Boarded, upstairs or below;
Engines throbbing, propellers churning,
Surprised when turning, at the view.

Across the water we found the Porthole,
A hostelry close by the north riverbank;
There we stayed till light was fading,
The ferry had come when we left for the ramp.
I looked down the river past Shields to the sea,
And saw a large freighter approaching downstream;
Two tugs kept it pinioned from starboard close in,
As they strove in the current to keep it on beam.

We boarded the ferry to watch as they passed,
The mass of the ship and the tugs pinned fast;
The lights on their tops cast a bright reflection
On the turbid waters, like a wall of lamps.
The swish of the bow wave, the swirl of the tide,
The thrust and power of those ships as they writhed;
They pushed up the river with a surging drive,
The Tzarevich from Valetta with two tugs beside.

THE ASH TREE

O indigenous Ash of ancient lineage,
The west wind sweeps your searching canopy,
Restless as Hecate amongst the foliage;
Survivor of the wildwood; now more solitary.
I look to see its grey lined bark,
With fissures crazed and opened vertically;
Wherein invertebrates hold the dark
And secret ways to remain in obscurity.
The Ash, its drooping boughs does shake
Its many clustered seeds from out the air;
Falling to earth in spins that wings do make:
Samaras sparking life in new territory.
Its nickname 'Venus of the woods'
Describes its contours and character perfectly.

THE ROWAN TREE

O Rowan Tree of mist and moor,
What earns you then that reputation,
Where, solitary across the lonely grassy slope,
You're known as 'Fairy Tree' by country folk?
Maybe the wind about your pinnate leaves,
Rustling and shimmering, suggests 'Quickbeam',
From Anglo-Saxon 'Cwic', where gusts do shake,
As though some fairy beckoned, so it would seem.
But more often 'Mountain Ash' is how you're known,
When you are found in fields and hills, bird sown.

And often you are found in city streets,
In central parks and gardens, once cameo guest;
But now accepted, without you incomplete,
Your autumn show of colour manifest.
Bunches of scarlet berries grow row by row,
Brightening each thoroughfare until they fall;
When thrushes come to feast before the sow,
Not caring if it be the shopping mall.
So many names: Also 'Witchen', and 'Witchwood',
Referring back to 'Fairy Tree', or should.

THE ENCHANTED FOREST TREE

O wild, enchanted forest tree,
Through your branches the free winds blow,
Wafting the scent of resin subtly
Across the path of a wanderer below.
That your fine, blue-green needles should hold
Candles to the open sky seems strange;
Or that your pine cones should be painted gold
So long after Autumn's colours change.

When the sun slips underhill,
Frosty crystals gather in fading light,
And through darkened woods the North wind chills
The thinning air into its very night.
Then comes the sound of laughter on the breeze,
In the empty wood there should be only the owl's cry;
But hide beneath the cover of these trees,
Upon the cushioned pine needles quietly lie.

The darkening forest closes around,
Now coloured baubles sparkle on the tree;
And tiny silver bells add their distinctive sound.
I wonder, how could all this be?
The tree assumes a strange, enchanted glow,
These decorations seem familiar now;
The same ones as on my tree at home.
I ran away as fast as I could go.

There is no cure for imagination's ways,
Fear stalks the dark and gloomy forest,
Though enchantment holds curiosity, which stays
Close to its genius, until understood.

NOW THE SWIFTS HAVE GONE

Now the swifts have gone,
Flown on the chill winds of Autumn
To the coasts of Africa,
Seeking their desert homes.
And you too are gone, my love,
Far from our cold Winter.
Salute then the coming Spring,
When the broad sun shines again,
And the screaming swifts
Are heard once more in our streets,
As they dart across the roofs
In wild excitement.
Then, my love, you too will return,
With your hair streaming in the warm wind,
Laughing in a music of happiness,
And smiling in our love.

Winner of the Scarborough Poetry Workshop Competition for 1987

FIELDING AT POINT

The ball came off the bat
Incredibly fast.
I was fielding close in at point;
I never saw it.
I shot out my left hand
In an involuntary gesture,
And in so doing,
Plucked the ball,
Like a plum,
Right out of the air.
It stuck in the palm of my hand.
No one but me
Knew I hadn't seen it,
And so I received
The most enthusiastic plaudit;
But not from the batsman,
Who guessed that I'd fluked it.

THE FIREWORK

It all started in McFee's bedroom one day,
When he made a device of his own;
He filled a cylinder with gunpowder,
And set it down on the floor.
He lit the fuse and watched by the door,
While it fizzed and spluttered to action.
The resultant explosion gave great satisfaction,
And his eyebrows were singed to a wisp.
But the floor took the worst,
The carpet was burst,
With a big black hole in the middle.
We came and we looked,
It was all very good,
And we thought it was time for a cracker.

McFee set to work in November,
With potassium nitrate, charcoal and sulphur.
He built a large firework
With speed and elastic,
And bound it round tightly with string.
We set out one night
With the monster held tight,
And a torch and some matches to light it.
Like fugitives we crept
While the village folk slept,
To the refuse dump, well secluded.
McFee went forward,
The device clutched awkward,
And settled it secure on the ground.
He lit the fuse at the second attempt,
And ran back to where we had halted.

The resultant explosion,
Caused quite a commotion,
The loudest we'd ever heard;
And the flash in the dark was no ordinary spark,
As lights went on down the road.
We thought of police, and without a word,
We took off and raced out of sight.
We ran through the fields as fast as we could,
And disappeared into the night.

Now McFee he works far away,
He doesn't make bombs any more;
And the memory of the big explosion,
That's left with the hole in the floor.

INCONGRUOUS

I saw it moving
In the middle distance,
White, between the houses;
Immense and incongruous,
Gliding slowly from left to right,
Defying the buildings as it went.

Running down the street,
I caught a glimpse of it,
Poking above rooftops;
Passing house ends,
Then street corners,
Relentless in its forward progress.

At last I found a gap;
I saw it clearly then, a funnel!
Then came a mast, a structure,
And finally a whole ship;
Sailing down the Tyne at Shields,
Coursing eastwards to the open sea,
Its railings lined with voyagers.
No one waved.

I felt a sense of elation,
Of beauty and of power.
I watched them go,
Sadly, gladly.

SPIRIT OF TREES

Worshippers of trees and spirits within
Favour oak, and when they can,
Cluster in those leafy glades,
By sacred pools and drooping shades;
And holding hands, dance around
The boles of oak, where these be found.
Upon their heads are garlands of flowers,
Night-scented stock and daisy chains;
And as they dance, they sing their songs,
Then clutch the tree and tell it all:
Those whispered secrets none should know,
Their triumphs and their wrongs.

THE SEA

Many times I searched its rocky pools
For small aquatic creatures reliant on the tide;
Or splashed around in sandy coves,
While chasing the darting flounder when espied.
Blustery winds would stir the oncoming waves,
Rolling and cresting in blue and greenish grey,
As I sat watching from some grassy bluff,
Observing the peeping orchids by Cayton Bay.
Sometimes I'd dash into the flying spray,
Gasping at the cold, swimming out intrepidly,
To revel in the waves' overpowering rush.
I saw those golden ships far out to sea,
Which plied their trades across the roads,
So lucky they, that I would join them if I could.

EARLY AUTUMN

Crows caw,
Harshly, hungrily.
A farm tractor
Ploughs the stubble
Into furrows;
Seagulls follow,
Picking worms
And grubs
Turned by the blade.
Sounds travel far
On still, crisp air.
The clickety-clack
Of a train on the track
Can be heard clearly
Far across the valley,
A mile away.
Bronze flowerheads
Scented like musk
Give a welcome show
On chrysanthemum plants.
A surfeit of plums
Is ripe for picking.
I tread cautiously
Where ground is slipping.
Dampness clings.
Autumn's here.

THE BULLFINCH, WELL MET

I heard a bird sing merrily
Upon my birthday at Walsden.
A quiet song I'd never heard before,
Sung to its mate, that paler, rose encore.
It was a lofty April day of cotton clouds
That drifted far above the Pennine Way.
Flowering shrubs adorned the hillside slopes,
Where I in coloured poems wrote my steeple day.
There was a fleeting flash of white
Across darkened hedge and undergrowth;
And then a bullfinch came in sight,
Lighting on a nearby twig.
Stout, robust, with crimson breast,
The black head stood out, poised and alert.
Here was the origin of that song,
That flashed a white wing and was gone.
Not often seen and seldom heard,
My birthday gift in song and bird.

ROUGH DEAL FOR THE GAS MASKS

*During the Second World War, the Government issued gas masks to
everyone living in the UK, children and babies included. These were for
use in the event of Germany attacking us with mustard gas. Fortunately
that did not happen, and most of the gas masks were thrown out. A few
remained.*

The war was over. It was that time when, as children,
We were free to roam wherever we wished,
So long as we got back home in time for meals.
We had gone up to the tip that day,
Two miles away, looking amongst
The junk for anything interesting.
I found three gas masks, and took them home.
I showed them proudly to my mother at the back door.
'Where did you get them from?'
She asked, with a horrified look on her face.
'From the tip', I replied, rather dismayed at
Her reaction. 'Well,' she said, 'Those masks
Were put in our dustbin last week, as the Germans
Won't be coming now. So you can just take them
All the way back to the tip.'
People have laughed at this little anecdote
Ever since, but it wasn't the coincidence
Of finding and retrieving our own gas masks
That amused them most.
I didn't take them back to the tip.
Instead, I sunk them in a marsh in a
Corner of Hippingstone field, not far away.

I thought that was a more appropriate
End for them, as I trod them in,
Thinking of Hitler and Himmler, no doubt!
Of course Mother didn't believe me
When I said I'd gone back to the tip.
I was far too quick!

THE BONFIRE

It was the first day of March.
I caught the smell of logfires burning,
Saw the seasons were slowly turning;
A strong wind blew across the waking land.
All the washing lines were empty,
Which had been pegged with clothes for drying,
But rain had fallen, and I took my chance
To build a bonfire; the lion's roar perchance.
I scrumpled news sheets into screws,
And placing them beneath thin twigs,
Lit the edge and stood to watch,
While acrid tongues engulfed the news.
Hot bright flames extended higher,
Fanned by wind which, ever drier,
Swept the blaze across the pile,
Consuming all in raging fire.

Smoke swirled up, got in my eyes;
Then stepping back, to my surprise
I thought I saw a lion crouching,
Watching me beyond the flames.
I stirred the blaze and poked around it
Until at length the fire subsided
Into a heap of glowing embers;
But I was pleased with that instead
Of all that rubbish piled up high

That with my leisure had collided.
Bright sparks lit up inside my mind
That I in words some new idea might find:
A woody smell clung to my clothes;
This was the lion's breath, so I supposed.

NIGHT SONG

Sometimes I hear her singing in the night,
A tune from long ago, remembered still.
Though indistinct, the melody floats across,
Bringing thoughts of home and friendships past.
All else asleep, no whisper stirs the house,
Only the west wind rustling in the trees.
Her happy memories are cast into the night,
And I, who share so many, hear them drifting by;
Unable to catch them, as in a dream, can fly.

When some weeks later, I lay in bed,
Half in, half out of sleep, my mind inert,
I found myself committed to a song.
Tuneless, wordless, the unmapped way
Gave out its strange refrain, all new,
And I too came to song by night,
In those margins of half-conscious thought.
But what was it I heard her sing?
I lie awake, waiting, that it might begin.

After J.M.W. Turner

CONKERS

I went looking for conkers up Stagshaw Bank,
On an Autumn day when the air was still.
Below the high stone wall I shuffled about
In the fallen leaves, searching for nowt.
Horse chestnut trees stretched out above,
Swaying and sighing, but nothing fell out.

So I shuffled about in the litter below,
Finding a conker and pocketing it so.
I looked at the wall, but it seemed very high,
And I couldn't get over, though I had a try.
I shuffled some more and got a reply,
Shuffle for shuffle, so I wondered why.

I did three shuffles and got three back;
I broke a twig; there came an echoing crack.
'Who's there?' I called, there was no reply,
So I jumped up the wall; no one was there.
As I walked away I didn't look round,
But I brought out the big fat conker I'd found.

BLUEBELL WOOD

From Aden Dene this little stream
Leads up the fields to Bluebell Wood.
Nameless, it wanders as in a dream
Past scenes of childhood; here I stood.
The aspen and the sleeping thorn
Droop low over waters meandering up
Through ripening wheat and waving corn,
Bordered by stitchwort and buttercup.
The wood itself is scarcely such,
But oh, so secret, no one knows.
On every side the meadows touch,
No road comes near and no one goes.
And here I am to write my poems,
Where peeps the wild rose from the hedge.
In nature's garden the wild bee drones,
And pleasing airs drift through the sedge.
Ash and oak about me stir,
Flights of fancy come nearby;
Mine to imagine and to wonder
Which to pick, and which let fly.
Let me wander o'er the green leas,
Brightly coloured flowers my thoughts;
Or lie amongst the scented bluebells,
In springy Juno's pleasant courts.
No maiden comes to lie beside me,
Nor smiling eyes fix and beguile me;
Company and wit inspire me,

Welcome those that seek and find me.
See the tiny willow warbler
Flit among the budding trees;
Its domed nest hidden in the grass
Where sheaves of fescue form a frieze.
Leave I now the Bluebell Wood,
My task is done, my poem writ.
Might I never come again,
May others find it still the same.

ALLEYWAYS OF OLD SCARBOROUGH

There's alleyways and narrow ways
By the Sandside Road;
Some of them's named,
Others are just postcode.
There's Bethel Place, and that wide street
By the Richard the Third;
Where the King came for a few days,
And he stayed there, so I've heard.
So if you're in Scarborough
Why don't you call in?
It's a diner with a public bar,
You could end here or begin.
If you walk to the car park,
There's Long Greece Steps to the side;
Climb up to the top,
And turn right: there beside
Is Burr Bank with the Flower-in-Hand
You can get a good view;
There's a mounted placard to a local artist,
Karl Hermann, and a copy painting too.
Below you there's Quay Street,
With Salmon Steps near the fair;
A short walk round the corner,
and the harbourside's there.
Then return by the Sandside Road,
Past trawlers moored next the quay;

And turn in by East Sandgate,
Away from the sea.
The Bolts is an alleyway
That's not often used;
It ends in a covered walkthrough
Where entry is refused.
So go by the Longroom Passage,
Conversely, it's very short;
Then on to the main road,
And you're back at the start.

A WINTER'S JOURNEY PAST PENDLE HILL

Pendle stood back, inscrutable, as I passed;
Its high round summit covered in snow,
That thick snow which falls fast,
Blown across the bleak fell tops,
To collect in deep, gleaming drifts;
Reflecting sunshine slanting low,
Which holds the discerning eye from far below.
Maybe in those old cotton towns no eye is raised
To admire the pristine beauty of Pendle's brow;
But certainly the traveller sees it, passing through,
And like myself, recalls some thrill from long ago:
A glimpse of Howgill Fells dusted in snow.
My road to Burnley lay close by Pendle Hill,
Whose summit brushes the clouds, majestic, sentinel.

COPPER PENNIES

We were waiting for trains
Two hundred yards from the gaping mouth
Of the tunnel. Nothing stirred.
A few hundred yards the other way
Lay Corbridge Station, and beyond that,
The track stretched straight as an arrow
For at least two miles.
We could see right down,
And I can remember now
The first sign of a train coming:
That distant black speck,
Taking absolutely ages to grow larger,
Until if you watched for long enough,
It would develop into a train.
Sometimes they stopped at the station,
But expresses came on through.
Nevertheless we didn't bother much
With eastbound traffic;
It was in the tunnel
That our chief interest lay.

When all was clear,
We walked out onto the track,
And placed copper pennies on the line.
We always looked at dates, to compare;
I never put a Victorian penny down.
The idea was to get them indented,
And examine the result for a laugh.
When we were ready, we left the track

And waited.

The first sign of an approaching train
Was the faint sound of shunting,
Growing ever louder, until suddenly
With a great 'Whoosh' the engine emerged
From the tunnel's mouth in a cloud of steam,
And bore down upon us at high speed.
Transfixed, I looked on,
Standing by the fence near the track,
As the monster approached down the line:
The Newcastle to Carlisle express,
Travelling at full speed, would pass close by,
Its massive weight clattering on the rails,
Throwing up steam and smoke at great pressure,
Red-hot coals falling on the track.
The driver saw us standing there,
And the engine let out a loud whistle,
Warning us to keep well away.
In a moment it had thundered past.
It didn't stop at the station;
Disappearing into the distance, it became a memory,
But we ran on the track to see
What had happened to our copper pennies:
All squashed and clearly ruined,
But we were quite happy at that.
Then we realised they might come
From the station to find us,
And we left with our flattened pennies,
A little poorer, but a lot wiser.

ESCAPE FROM DOGS

Lying flat, face down upon the riverbank,
Looking upstream across the pebbles;
I watched the water, sparkling, flowing,
And a grey wagtail hopping, flitting.

Then I heard them, shouting, running,
Ever nearer to me, searching;
Poking bushes as they went,
Dogs were sniffing for my scent.

I rolled sideways into the cold river,
Before they came in view. I knew
To creep in deeper, ever steeper,
Hold my breath and keep quite still.

My lungs were bursting; I rolled right over,
Took a breath and popped back under.
Dogs were circling, sneezing, wheezing,
I knew what caused it; they went away.

Soaking wet, I snatched a quick glance.
The bank was clear, I took my chance;
Crawled ashore with clothes all dripping,
Retrieved my pepper spray from the rushes
That I had squirted on the grass.

Shivering, chattering,
Sniffing and sneezing,
Like the police dogs,
But for a different reason;
I covered my tracks with pepper spray,
Up and hopped it, ran away.

THE ELDER

Be it bush or tree? Now that's the rub;
No smaller tree nor bigger shrub
Does grace the splendour of the hedge,
Nor line the moorland's rugged edge.
Discreetly the elder grows wherever wanted,
In gaps or spaces, seldom vaunted.
Come May, it paints the waysides bright
With strange-scented* blossoms in corymbs of white,
That with a magic brush turn into green berries,†
And then in Autumn to purple jewels of the night.
Once poor country folk would gather them for fruit,
But now the mistle thrush claims this as his pursuit.
Pause then to drink of elderberry wine,
Or elderflower, that idle moments be sublime.

*Strange-scented – Some do not like it.
†A reference to the pollinating brush used by horticulturists, often in greenhouses.

THE ROMAN STONE

The stone
Had remained in situ
For nearly two thousand years.
It had been placed in position
By Roman military engineers,
As part of the stonework
To support a small bridge,
Where the Stanegate crossed
The Corburn near Corstopitum.
It was low down
Near the water's edge,
Faced, and cuboid.
The turf and clay
Had overlapped and hidden it
From view for centuries.

I was aware of its presence,
Having wandered by many times,
And was interested in such matters;
So I decided to clear the grass,
And get a better look at it.
It was a nice stone,
Well-shaped, and selected
Specifically for its purpose.
However, to my dismay,
When next I passed that way,
The stone was gone.
Someone passing by,

Not knowing of its significance,
Had removed the stone.
There was now no way of telling
Exactly where the Stanegate had passed.
After all those years,
My actions had betrayed the stone's
Presence to the world.

I saw the stone again.
It was in a local garden.
One night I took it back to the stream,
And put it where it belonged.
Perhaps they'll think a River God
Did it, and leave it be.
I haven't been back to see.

WINDER

Water comes cascading down
The steep hillside gully
Between Winder and Crook,
Descending in tiny waterfalls and rapids,
Tumbling fitfully over its stony bed
To reach the River Rawthey far below.
The banks of Settlebeck Gill
Are lined with oak, birch and alder,
Continuing up until they reach
The gate in the dry stone wall,
At the foot of Winder Hill.
Beyond that neither tree nor bush grows
And the path follows the gill.
After a short walk you leave the track,
Striking left hard up Winder's side,
Straining muscle and limb at each step.
Towards the summit the gradient eases,
Until eventually you reach the cairn,
A loose pile of assorted stones;
I always found one to add to the heap.
From the top of Winder on a clear day,
The valley and Sedbergh lie far below,
And neighbouring hills loom large,
Their lonely grassy tops never change;
Have been like that for thousands of years.
The view is your reward,
The way down quick and untoward.

GREENFINCHES

The south wind rustles through fading leaves
On the lime tree outside my window;
Leaves turned yellow-green, thinning out.
It's mid-October, the greenfinches are long gone.
I remember when they came in February;
There were no leaves on the tree then,
That tree on a suburban road
In a seaside town somewhere in England.
You could see greenfinches perched on topmost twigs,
Facing the hazy sun, uttering wild calls, 'Zwee,'
Through their short, stubby beaks,
With bursts of notes and trills,
Full of exuberance and joy of coming Spring.
Not long there, then up and off again,
Visiting each favourite tree, their territory.
Now the tree is empty.
But come next February they'll be back,
Back to this same street, this same tree;
My tree: their tree.

DOWN PENDLE HILL

My love she lives near Pendle hill,
Snowdrop wild and daffodil;
Much higher than the Great Whin Sill,
Through swinging-gate and over stile.

Climb it on a wild March day,
Mountain ash and heather spray;
The wind will blow your cares away,
Posies red and rosemary.

My love she lives in Burnley town.
From Pendle's summit looking down,
See a patchwork quilt for eiderdown,
And cotton mills gone tumbledown.

I come from far to see my love,
A fresh wind sweeps across the hill;
Striding down from Pendle's high crown,
I knock-a-door and enter in.

WADERS

Hungrily they search the grainswept day,
Wading in the foaming shallows expectantly;
Detached from many raucous gulls,
That soar and cry above the spray
Along the sands of Scarborough Bay.

As breaking waves rush in to shore,
So does the sanderling busily engage
Upon darting at the bubbly edge,
In little groups of three or four,
Or on occasion, several more.

And in a separate place nearby,
The turnstone plays at hide and seek,
Prodding with its short sharp beak
For any food it might espy
On lifting stones, that underlie.

Lucky the observer who might see
Those denizens upon the beach:
Oystercatchers in black and white,
With legs and beaks in orange bright,
Which makes a most effective sight.

Further down the windswept beach
See other waders, more wild and wary:
Redshanks, as the name implies;
And curlews with long downturned beaks
That probe where others cannot reach.

Walkers push on relentlessly,
Taking the air along the front;
While I, who come to look at birds,
Adjust my binoculars to focus first,
And set my afternoon down in words.

CORVIDAE

That bright-eyed bird the carrion crow
Is not so daft as he might seem.
If there's some trick he doesn't know,
He'll work it out and hatch a scheme.

The birdfeeder is to him a challenge,
Conveniently dangling from some tree.
Watch him perch upon the top
And peck until the string breaks free.

The magpie's gift is all for taking,
Bright jewel or bird's egg he'll not pass by.
His domed nest secured at twice the making,
Know him pied with rattling cry.

By contrast, the jackdaw's call is "yak",
He wears his ruff in shades of grey.
He'll nest within a chimney stack,
Nor sooty sweep will him dismay.

Who seeks the brightly-coloured jay
May find him in vibrant Todmorden town.
Look for him sometime, as gifts the day,
Where Walsden Water comes rushing down.

The raven comes with massive beak,
Some moorish hill or crag his lair.
See him soar above mountain peak,
Circling on thermals of rising air.

But at Tower of London the raven stays;
If he should go, then England falls.
They've clipped his wings to curb his ways,
He's tourists' wag within four walls.

VICTOR AND CORY

Part A

I lay asleep in Bluebell Wood,
Amongst the grass by that small stream;
It was high noon in early June,
In the year of our Lord Nineteen Fifteen.

A summer breeze stirred in the trees,
I sensed the hum of wild bees droning.
The cascades of a wood wren's song
Shimmered in the air, that I be gone.

Too late! There came the distant drum
Of horses' hooves approaching fast.
I woke, and wondered who it was,
And rose to watch them as they passed.

I walked up through the tangled wood,
Peering out between the leaves;
And by the edge I stopped and stood,
Quite still and hidden by the trees.

Across the hill and into view
Came two black horses, large and strong;
A lady rode upon the one,
The other, riderless, followed on.

She saw me standing in the wood,
And came across to speak to me.
I stepped right out into the field,
And then she asked, 'Might you be free?'

She said she rode to Appleby,
To sell her horses at the fair,
And asked if I would ride with her,
For company, upon the spare.

I saw the horse was fully saddled,
Said I would, and up I got;
I had the strangest feeling then,
That discretion lacked, and I should not.

She said she was the Lady Lara,
Around her hair a golden band;
Glittering rings with rubies and diamonds
Sparkled brightly on her hand.

We crossed the fields and open moors,
Past cottages and bleak farmsteads.
Little more she spoke until
We reached the hill near Allenheads.

Here we rested the great black horses,
Which grazed the lush grass upon the edges;
The barren moor stretched out before us,
County Durham lay ahead.

Still she spoke but little to me,
I seemed to sense that she was troubled;
And so I asked her what it was:
She said she wished the war was ended.

Past Whitestone House and over Lamb's Head,
We travelled on to Dufton Fell;
Coming down past Keisley and Flakebridge,
To spend the night in rooms at Burrells.

Next morning we rode on to Appleby,
Where all was busy at the fair.
Gypsy caravans and smoky campsites
Covered the spare ground everywhere.

All along the highways and byways
Came travelling men with horses trotting;
Testing them for any defects,
Which to my mind took some spotting.

Up and down the busy main street,
Back and forth the horses went;
Accompanied by their hopeful owners,
Some were sold, others spent.

Then army trucks came into town,
And stopped near to the market square.
Soldiers alighted, asking questions,
Buying fit horses for the war.

Lady Lara was quite distraught,
Her horses would now go to war, alas!
The soldiers bought her two black horses,
Led them off to our distress.

Discreetly we followed the horses down
To the railway yard not far away,
Where they were loaded onto waggons,
To start their journey that same day.

This, she told me, was what she had feared,
And was the reason that she took them
To Appleby Fair, to sell to gypsies,
Thinking they would be safe once there.

Lady Lara gave me more money
Than I had thought I must have earned,
And I set off by train without her;
To my home town I then returned.

Part B

Next year I received my call-up papers,
When I was living down at Shields.
I joined the army with many others,
Fought with them for three long years.

Many bullets passed close by me,
Many shells exploding shook me;
Mustard gas blew just beyond me,
Only nicks and scratches touched me.

Lucky as I was to survive all this,
Many more fell dead nearby;
And I, who fought as hard as any,
Wondered at how I did not die.

But came the day when peace descended
On the embattled trenches of the Somme;
And though I had to stay in Belgium,
The dangers of open war were gone.

Eventually we received our orders,
The Durham Light Infantry were to return.
We embarked for Portsmouth, then on to London,
Pending the day we were stood down.

Still in uniform, and free to wander,
I walked through London's crowded streets;
Everything seemed new and wonderful,
Different from the way I'd lived.

There was excitement in the air,
A coach swept past towards the palace,
Followed by the Sovereign's escort.
I edged to the front where I could see.

The trees right down the Mall were newly green,
With dappled sunshine slanting through the leaves,
To fall as speckled patterns on the road.
Many Union Jacks were fluttering in the breeze.

Above the top end of the Mall unseen,
A massed band and many troops were gathering,
Which now around the corner came,
The sunlight on their bayonets glistening.

The band played 'British Grenadiers',
As out it swung from Horseguards Parade,
Into the long avenue of the Mall,
Beneath the green trees casting shade.

The crowd went frantic when they saw this,
Surely London's greatest spectacle;
And down it came past all the sentries,
The massed bands of The Guards Regiments.

Behind them marched five hundred soldiers,
With scarlet tunics and bearskin hats:
The Grenadiers, the Coldstream Guards;
Then Irish, Scots and Welsh in turn.

At the rear of this procession
Came two black horses bearing officers:
A major of the Grenadier Guards,
And the adjutant, who was a captain.

Then it happened all at once:
The two black horses stopped and walked across.
They came to me with nostrils flaring,
Their great black eyes were fiercely glaring.

'Steady there,' the major said,
As up to me those horses came.
In amongst the crowds of people,
What was it, that I was not the same?

And then I got it, held my hands up,
These were Lady Lara's horses:
Those years ago at Appleby Fair,
They remembered I was there.

'They recognise you,' the major said,
Both officers were now grinning broadly;
'I know them,' said I, and told them briefly
What it was from where I stood.

'Come and see us at the barracks,
And you can ride them if you wish.'
They told me where, and off they cantered,
Their hooves were drumming; my memory switched.

Long, long ago, as I lay sleeping
In Bluebell Wood, beside that stream,
It was the sound of hooves drumming
That stirred me from a strange daydream.

There it started, Lady Lara speaking,
Asking me to ride with her;
I remembered her, on that June morning,
In London's Mall I felt despair.

But I imagined her beside me,
Rings and gemstones on her hand;
A golden chain hung on her garments,
The Lady from Northumberland.

And when I went up to the barracks
The next day, in the morning sun,
The major and the captain saw me,
Told me what it was they'd done.

They'd traced the Lady Lara for me,
And she had come the long way down;
Out she came to thank me gladly,
We were pleased to meet again.

And so the Grenadier major and captain
Accompanied us to the horses' stables;
Where Victor and Cory went ecstatic
To see the two of us again.

The horses stayed within the Corps,
They had learned the ways of ceremonial;
And in so doing, escaped the war
That had so nearly been their undoing.

The Lady married the Grenadier captain,
And went to live in London's Mayfair.
I went home to the North of England,
Lucky was I to escape the war.

Thus it is we make our friendships,
Fate decides whom we will choose;
Man and horse share that one destiny:
Who will win, and who will lose.

CHANCE

Sometimes I chance upon you in city streets,
Maybe in wild, inclement weather;
But if in passing, your Gallic smile greets
My own sanguine thoughts, then come whatever,
We'll be together, even under umbrella.
For those few moments we can exchange our news;
On crowded pavements, with people rushing through.
Walking down past bus stops with long queues,
We make our workplace exits and adieus.

On occasion, when I pick up my office phone,
It's you that's there, the telephone operator;
And suddenly I find I'm not so much alone,
But chanced upon my future alter-mater.
And so we have a laugh before I make my call;
Our busy lives, so full, have glanced upon each other
Once again, maybe will gel together, in any weather.
Come the day I'll phone you up and ask,
No matter rain nor sun, if you will chance your all.

SEA HORSES

I saw them dashing through the wild surf,
A group of fiery horses let loose to run;
Like thoroughbreds racing across the turf,
Their hooves flashed as silver in the morning sun.
The beach was clear as they sped,
Straight down the beady edge where waves rushed through;
Raiders and waders as one turned and fled,
And the splash and the spray sparkled and flew.
I followed them on with my eyes as they went,
All the way down till I saw them no more;
To gallop, then canter, until they were spent:
And the tide washed their prints from the shore

THE TWO-HEADED PENNY

Would you find me a two-headed penny?
The shops say they havn't got any.
But they had a tenpenny,
There can't be many
With two heads instead of the one.
When I went, they said it had gone,
They were sorry, it must have been spent;
Or at least handed out in small change,
Though I wasn't too clear what they meant.

Now there was
A two-headed penny;
How it got in my change
I don't know.
So I spun it for luck,
Called 'Heads', did a duck,
But it rolled in a crack
And got stuck

Now it showed neither head, nor tails,
It was wedged in a vertical position;
So who do you think won the toss?
A draw was my logical conclusion.
It does not always follow to form
That your two-headed penny will win;
For as you can see from the norm,
Who calls 'Heads' first will win on the spin.

THE CRAB APPLE TREE

In May its blossom stands out clearly in the new green hedge,
Bunched bracts on every bough in pink and dappled white;
Visited by many bees and other insects from the edge
Of bordering fields, that on the scattered flowers alight.
Malus Sylvestris is our native Crab Apple tree,
Botanically distinct from specimens of a cultivated ancestry
In that its shoots are typically found pointed and thorny.
Remembered since childhood, still held in awe,
Wild apple gives some special presence to where it grows:
That mysterious space where falls in Autumn a bitter store
Of tiny fruits that lie untouched where Nature sows;
Just once might strike a lucky pip from out an apple core.
Here perchance the linnet comes to sing his song:
When Spring is out and Summer comes, he'll soon be gone.

CALL HEADS

How much do you think it would cost
To buy a two-headed penny?
>> I went to the shop,
>> But it got put on stop
When they said they hadn't got any.

But they had a two-headed tenpenny.
They hadn't acquired very many;
>> So I bought one for show,
>> Stuck it deep down below,
And took the bus to Kilkenny.

Now I hadn't got very much money,
And you'll think I'm just being funny;
>> But they wanted the fare,
>> And it just wasn't there,
It was ten pence short on the tally.

So I reached down below in my pocket,
And brought out the two-headed tenpenny.
>> I said I would toss it,
>> Called 'Heads' and they lost it,
And now I'm back in Kilkenny.

I've still got my bright new tenpenny,
But of cash I haven't got any.
>> I'm off to the pub,
>> With a spin and a shove,
To see if I make any money.

ROSAMUND

She lived within a castle's strong stone walls,
The Lady Rosamund of Northumberland, highly esteemed;
Suitors came from far on amorous calls,
But none she fancied much, or so it seemed.

Her workroom was high up the tallest tower,
Where with her ladies she sewed embroidery;
And looking out upon the picturesque countryside,
She traced that which she saw in tapestry.

Below the tower, the dusty road ran past
Across fine rural lands which stretched afar;
Many times she gazed down when travellers passed,
From her vantage point in the perpendicular.

Thus it was until the Summer came,
When with her ladies she would ride across the leas.
Her horse was strong and swift: Jerico his name,
Whose temperament was calm, that never failed to please.

They raced their horses fast across the fields,
Galloping those thoroughbreds at furious speed.
Always Jerico came first and others last,
No rival horse could challenge him for lead.

Unexpectedly Rosamund decided early one day
To take some friends into the Cheviot Hills;
And as they would be perhaps a week away,
To include those staff with necessary skills.

They travelled out to Wooler and stopped close by,
Making camp upon a grassy slope to spend the night;
Then, starting next morning, they passed through Earle,
And after Middleton Hall, the Cheviots were in sight.

Following the Harthorpe Burn which took them on their route,
The ground began to rise upon the stony track;
With Hedgehope Hill and Cheviot lying close ahead,
Steely Crag and Rockside were at their back.

The party went up Long Lee with its stunted trees,
And took the path to Cheviot in single file;
Lady Rosamund was riding upon Jerico,
Her ladies and the support group came behind.

At dusk they camped upon the slopes of Cheviot,
Close by the summit of England's northern hill;
Made fires and settled down to spend the night,
Huddled up against the blustery upland chill.

It was here that events took a strange new turn:
Sometime in the small hours before dawn,
The party were woken by the middle watch,
Alerting them to the sound as of a distant horn.

Beyond West Hill, over towards Easter Tor,
There came the drumming of horses' hooves;
The sight of growing unnatural light,
That lit their faces, curiously flickering in the cold night.

Closer it came upon the terrified ensemble,
Until, drawing near, three horsemen appeared:
The Riders of the Violet Stray, that rode the skies
By night and day, that never stopped nor would
Not stay, until all evil on the Earth
Was driven out and gone away.

The riders all wore crowns of gold,
That glistened with sparkling jewels around.
Their hard eyes glinted down with fury and steel,
Their horses snorted and pawed the ground.

Said Theodar: 'Greetings from the Violet Stray.
Roam we ever where we may. Yonder Horse
Who is he? We wish to have him if we may.'
So saying, he indicated Jerico, the Lady's Bay.

Lady Rosamund stepped forward from her group:
'The horse is Jerico; come rain or shine,
You cannot have him, he is mine.'
So saying, she mounted Jerico in fury and alarm.

Then rode forward the second of the Riders
Of the Violet Stray: Princess Ingrid spoke:
'We must take your Jerico; until we have him
We won't go. Name your price and we will pay.'

But Lady Rosamund, while inwardly badly shaken,
Steadfastly refused to dismount and negotiate.
'I will never sell my horse, not for gold will he be taken.'
And she sat there in defiance most resolute.

And so came forward the third rider of the Stray,
Prince Dagmar. He said 'If you will not sell
Your horse, will you marry me and come with us?
That will mean leaving your earthly comfortable life,
And riding on Jerico wherever we go.
Come with us now, and make it so.'

Lady Rosamund looked at her friends,
Smiled sadly and said farewell.
Here was an offer she could not refuse,
Where it would take her, no one could tell.

So she turned back to Dagmar, said she would go,
And she rode across to be by his side.
In an instant she was caught in the violet glow;
With a crown on her head, she became his bride.

The stars they twinkled in the cold night air,
Over Cheviot Hill in England's far North.
And the riders departed from where they had come,
To combat with evil throughout all of the Earth.

The rest of the party wandered back home,
Not knowing, nor caring, what should be done;
For the lady was gone, but who would believe them?
So they said she rode off for her own good reason.

Her ladies went back to their room up the tower,
To sew and embroider, the same as before;
But they missed her in chatter and they missed her in smiles,
Yet she left a reminder to keep them awhiles:
For there in the fabric of her fine tapestry cloth
Was the figure of Rosamund on Jerico wove.
On her head was a crown, in her hand was a sword,
And Prince Dagmar in violet, by her side he rode.

CELTIC POEM

Here I stand in silvery pale moonlight,
Looking out across Tintagel's rocky spur;
Its rugged outline silhouetted
Against glimmering sea and open sky.
Nearby a buddleia, aromatic as India, scents the night,
Reaching like a lantern tower to heaven.
Above, the sparkling prospect of the galaxy
Is studded out with magnitudes and planets.
There are no shadows here, nor shades
Of things past, only the unknown, beckoning.

And that other silent one, the land,
Will speak if only you believe,
Waiting on the slept windswept coastal
Path in the deep fallen night.
Stretch down your fingers to the earth,
Listen for a faint cry
Very far away, calling.
The Mother Earth is speaking to you
In the language of our ancestors.
Yes, we understand, are not afraid.